Bond
No.1 for exam success

Skills

Spelling and Vocabulary

10–11 years

OXFORD
UNIVERSITY PRESS

OXFORD
UNIVERSITY PRESS

Great Clarendon Street, Oxford, OX2 6DP, United Kingdom

Oxford University Press is a department of the University of Oxford. It furthers the University's objective of excellence in research, scholarship, and education by publishing worldwide. Oxford is a registered trade mark of Oxford University Press in the UK and in certain other countries

Text © Michellejoy Hughes 2015

Illustrations © Oxford University Press 2015

The moral rights of the author have been asserted

First published in 2015

All rights reserved. No part of this publication may be reproduced, stored in a retrieval system, or transmitted, in any form or by any means, without the prior permission in writing of Oxford University Press, or as expressly permitted by law, by licence or under terms agreed with the appropriate reprographics rights organization. Enquiries concerning reproduction outside the scope of the above should be sent to the Rights Department, Oxford University Press, at the address above.

You must not circulate this work in any other form and you must impose this same condition on any acquirer

British Library Cataloguing in Publication Data
Data available

978-0-1927-9381-2

10 9 8 7 6 5 4 3 2 1

Paper used in the production of this book is a natural, recyclable product made from wood grown in sustainable forests. The manufacturing process conforms to the environmental regulations of the country of origin.

Printed in China

Acknowledgements

Cover illustrations: Lo Cole

Although we have made every effort to trace and contact all copyright holders before publication this has not been possible in all cases.
If notified, the publisher will rectify any errors or omissions at the earliest opportunity.

Links to third party websites are provided by Oxford in good faith and for information only. Oxford disclaims any responsibility for the materials contained in any third party website referenced in this work.

Bond Skills Spelling and Vocabulary 10–11

Unit 1

A Can you match each of your words with their definitions? Use a line to join them up. [16]

1	Twirl	Braided hair or thread.
2	Bridal	Fantastic.
3	Plaits	My mother's or father's brother.
4	Blank	A place of worship.
5	Grateful	To twist or spin.
6	Laundry	Wedding, marriage.
7	Powerful	Community or communal.
8	Social	A material.
9	Wonderful	A missing space.
10	Selfish	Appreciative.
11	Claim	Fashion.
12	Plastic	Washing.
13	Uncle	Strong.
14	Style	Drag, pull, heave.
15	Temple	Not generous or thoughtful.
16	Lug	To make a statement.

B If we put all of these words in alphabetical order, which three words would come first? [3]

1 _____ 2 _____ 3 _____

> 💡 **Helpful Hint**
> A quick way of sorting a list of mixed words into alphabetical order is to first divide the list into half: A–M and N–Z. Now divide each half into roughly half again (A–F, G–M and N–S, T–Z). With manageable chunks it is now much easier to solve each little group.

Word list:
Blank
Bridal
Claim
Grateful
Laundry
Lug
Plaits
Plastic
Powerful
Selfish
Social
Style
Temple
Twirl
Uncle
Wonderful

19

Unit 1

Bond Skills Spelling and Vocabulary 10–11

Alien

Auntie

Belief

Brilliant

Carried

Cushion

Fields

Grief

Interview

Ion

Nightie

Period

Relief

Riot

Superior

View

C All of the words in your list are here but the letters have been replaced with numbers. Can you work out which letter each number represents to solve the puzzle? [18]

D All of these words have an 'i' in them but can you find the two words that make another word when you take the 'i' away? [2]

1 _____   2 _____

E Can you find the three words that have an 'i' as the third letter of the word? [3]

1 _____   2 _____   3 _____

💡 **Helpful Hint**

Remember that when an 'i' and 'e' are next to each other in a word, the 'i' usually comes before an 'e' unless it is after a 'c'.

23

Bond Skills Spelling and Vocabulary 10–11

Unit 1

F All of the words in your list fit into the grid below. Can you use the clues to complete the crossword? [16]

Across

2 A question
4 To stand in a line
7 Not gas or solid
8 Paste or stick
11 Petrol
12 A woodland animal
14 Cookies
15 A road or walkway

Down

1 Mean
3 A drink made from fruit
5 A belt around the world
6 Four equal-sided shape
9 Worth something
10 A problem
11 Flows easily
13 To save

Avenue

Biscuits

Cruel

Equator

Fluid

Fuel

Glue

Issue

Juice

Liquid

Query

Queue

Rescue

Square

Squirrel

Valuable

16

Unit 1

Bond Skills Spelling and Vocabulary 10–11

Alter

Corner

Crater

Customer

Danger

Disaster

Helicopter

Hover

Lobster

Number

Partner

Prefer

Quiver

Register

Splinter

Together

G Each of the words in your list are here as anagrams. That means that the letters of each word are all jumbled up. Can you put them into the correct order to spell each word? [16]

1 Treal _____
2 Reviqu _____
3 Ronrec _____
4 Creatr _____
5 Grande _____
6 Merbun _____
7 Preefr _____
8 Bolster _____

9 Orvhe _____
10 Pernart _____
11 Comerust _____
12 Thegetro _____
13 Printles _____
14 Thepolicer _____
15 Greetsir _____
16 Stairsed _____

H Which of your words mean the following: [6]

1 Hazard _____
2 A tiny sliver of wood _____
3 A client _____
4 To have a favourite option _____
5 To change _____
6 Catastrophe _____

> **Helpful Hint**
>
> All of these words end in 'er'. Although some words do end in 're' and 'ar', it is more common for the word to end in 'er'. So if you hear the 'r' sound and you are unsure of the spelling, it is always worth trying 'er' first.

Recap 6

Bond Skills Spelling and Vocabulary 10–11

Unit 2

A All the words in your list are in the word search. Once you have found them all, the remaining letters spell out a message. [17]

1 What is the message? _____

D	E	S	C	R	I	P	T	I	O	N	S
E	A	T	T	R	A	C	T	I	O	N	E
C	O	N	V	E	R	S	A	T	I	O	N
O	P	R	O	T	E	C	T	I	O	N	S
R	E	C	E	P	T	I	O	N	E	N	A
A	R	D	I	R	E	C	T	I	O	N	T
T	A	T	T	E	N	T	I	O	N	D	I
I	T	I	N	V	E	N	T	I	O	N	O
O	I	N	F	O	R	M	A	T	I	O	N
N	O	W	C	O	M	M	O	T	I	O	N
I	N	S	T	R	U	C	T	I	O	N	I
T	C	E	L	E	B	R	A	T	I	O	N
H	T	I	S	E	C	T	I	O	N	O	N

Attention
Attraction
Celebration
Conversation
Commotion
Decoration
Description
Direction
Information
Instruction
Invention
Operation
Protection
Reception
Section
Sensation

B What is the root word of the following words? [8]

1 Conversation _____   5 Invention _____
2 Decoration _____   6 Celebration _____
3 Description _____   7 Operation _____
4 Direction _____   8 Protection _____

💡 **Helpful Hint**

When a word ends in 'e', we usually remove the 'e' before adding the 'tion' ending.

25

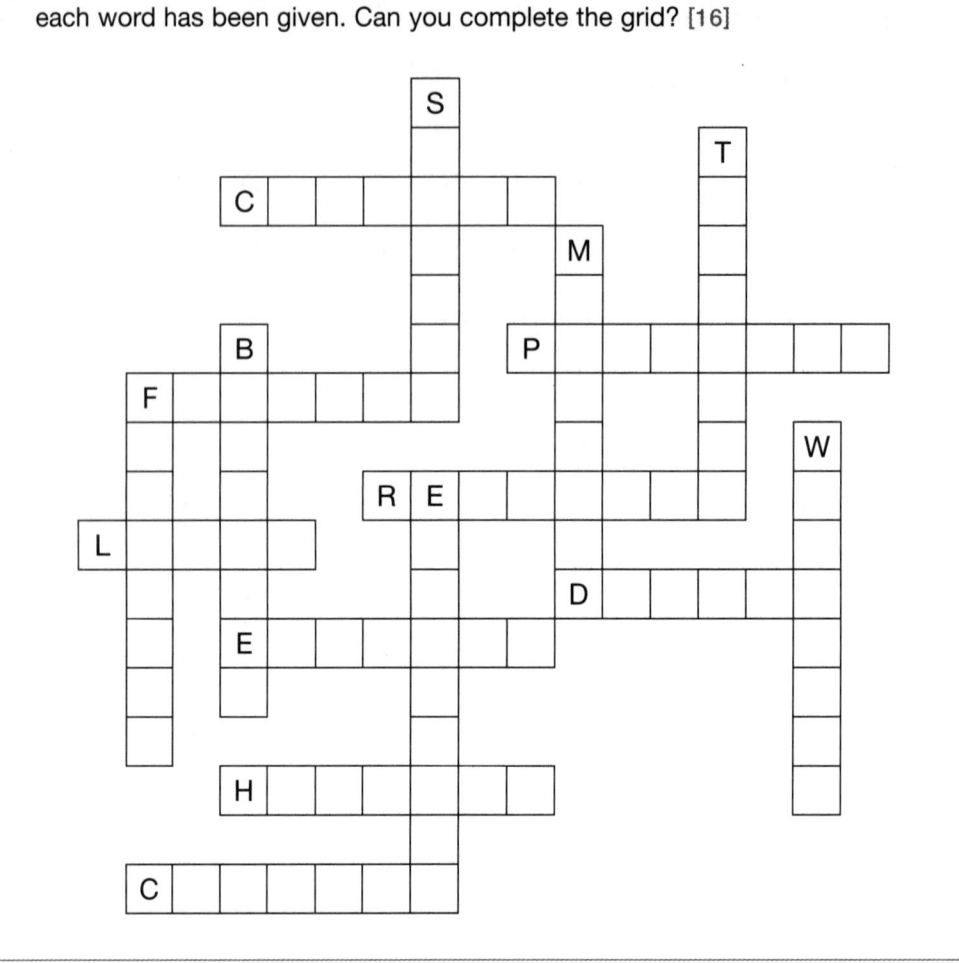

Unit 2

Bond Skills Spelling and Vocabulary 10–11

Word list:
- Bothered
- Climbed
- Covered
- Dodged
- Encrusted
- Entered
- Finished
- Frowned
- Haunted
- Lined
- Murdered
- Produced
- Returned
- Striped
- Tortured
- Wandered

C All of the words in your list are hidden in this grid. To help you, the first letter of each word has been given. Can you complete the grid? [16]

D Which of your words has these smaller words hidden in them? [8]

1. Own _____
2. Bed _____
3. And _____
4. Her _____
5. She _____
6. Rip _____
7. Urn _____
8. Over _____

💡 **Helpful Hint**

Most of the time, if a word ends in 'e', to show the past tense we just add 'd' but for words ending in any other letters, we add 'ed'.

Unit 2

Bond Skills Spelling and Vocabulary 10–11

E All of the words in your list are here but the letters have been replaced by numbers. Can you work out which letter each number represents to fill in the grid? [17]

A		M	
B		N	
C		O	
E		P	
G		R	6
I		S	
J		T	
K		U	
L		V	

F Which of your words mean the following? [8]

1 Used to see the night sky. _____

2 A break. _____

3 A small flow of liquid. _____

4 A family member. _____

5 Can be seen. _____

6 A gentle bend. _____

7 To find the answer. _____

8 Used to speak. _____

Curve

Joke

Negative

Pause

Positive

Prove

Relative

Repulsive

Savage

Solve

Telescope

Translate

Trickle

Visible

Voice

Volume

25

9

Unit 2

Bond Skills Spelling and Vocabulary 10–11

Almond

Answered

Arid

Crowd

Descend

Hatred

Hind

Humid

Overjoyed

Poked

Record

Reward

Timid

Visited

Wand

Wondered

G Once you have found all of the words in your list in the word search, the remaining letters spell out a message. [17]

1 What is the message? _____

D	E	S	C	E	N	D	A	T	O	H
A	R	H	I	N	D	H	N	V	V	E
R	E	W	A	R	D	A	S	I	E	H
I	C	A	L	E	N	T	W	S	R	U
D	O	N	M	P	D	R	E	I	J	M
L	R	D	O	O	E	E	R	T	O	I
T	D	T	N	K	E	D	E	E	Y	D
W	O	N	D	E	R	E	D	D	E	R
C	R	O	W	D	T	I	M	I	D	D

H Which of your words mean the following? [8]

1 Thought   _____

2 Back   _____

3 Magic stick   _____

4 Very dry   _____

5 A sweet nut   _____

6 Replied   _____

7 A large group   _____

8 Extremely happy _____

25

Recap

Bond Skills Spelling and Vocabulary 10–11

Unit 3

A Can you add one of the words in your list into each space so that each sentence makes sense? [16]

1. The wind blew _____ causing little effect to the leaves on the trees.

2. I have a _____ certificate showing the wedding of my great grandparents.

3. There was only one _____ travelling on the bus.

4. We baked a _____ cake for tea.

5. It was _____ of Zara to share her sweets with everyone.

6. I placed the butter in the _____ to keep it cool.

7. There were five birds perched on the window _____ .

8. The white paper is perfect for _____ or everyday printing.

9. It was a real _____ to reach the apples at the top of the tree.

10. The supple gymnast was extremely _____ .

11. We receive our _____ through food.

12. The railway _____ was full of passengers.

13. We pulled into the _____ forecourt to fill the car with petrol.

14. The angry head teacher was on a _____ .

15. I love to eat my _____ with cream and sugar on it.

16. Hermes was known as the _____ who served the Greek gods.

Agile
Carriage
Challenge
Energy
Fridge
Garage
General
Generous
Gently
Ledge
Marriage
Messenger
Passenger
Porridge
Rampage
Sponge

💡 Helpful Hint

All of these words have a soft 'g' which makes it sound like a 'j'. Remember that when you sound out a word, any 'j' sound may be spelt with a 'g' or 'dg'.

Unit 3

Bond Skills Spelling and Vocabulary 10–11

Berries

Bodies

Bunnies

Daisies

Elves

Enemies

Families

Ladies

Memories

Mummies

Noises

Ourselves

Replies

Senses

Soldiers

Vegetables

24

B Can you write the singlular form of the words in your list? [16]

1 Elves _____   9   Enemies _____
2 Families _____   10 Ladies _____
3 Mummies _____   11 Memories _____
4 Vegetables _____   12 Bodies _____
5 Noises _____   13 Senses _____
6 Bunnies _____   14 Berries _____
7 Daisies _____   15 Soldiers _____
8 Replies _____   16 Ourselves _____

C Which of your words mean the following? [8]

1 The people we are related to _____
2 Foods like carrots and sprouts _____
3 People in the army _____
4 Soft fruits _____
5 Answers _____
6 Rabbits _____
7 Mothers _____
8 Foes _____

Helpful Hint

When we pluralise a word ending in an 'f' we usually remove the 'f' and add 'ves'.
When we pluralise a word ending in a 'y', we usually remove the 'y' and add 'ies'.

Bond Skills Spelling and Vocabulary 10–11

Unit 3

D) All of the words from your list fit into the grid. Can you use the clues to complete the grid? [16]

Across

1. People from Germany
3. To be very cold
6. All together
8. A link
9. People from Italy
13. Someone with no parents
14. A mark
15. Our bones

Down

1. To have become larger
2. A purpose
4. A point of view
5. Where the sky joins the land
7. Current style
10. To hear
11. A worry
12. A large house

Chain

Concern

Fashion

Frozen

German

Grown

Horizon

Italian

Listen

Mansion

Opinion

Orphan

Reason

Skeleton

Stain

Unison

16

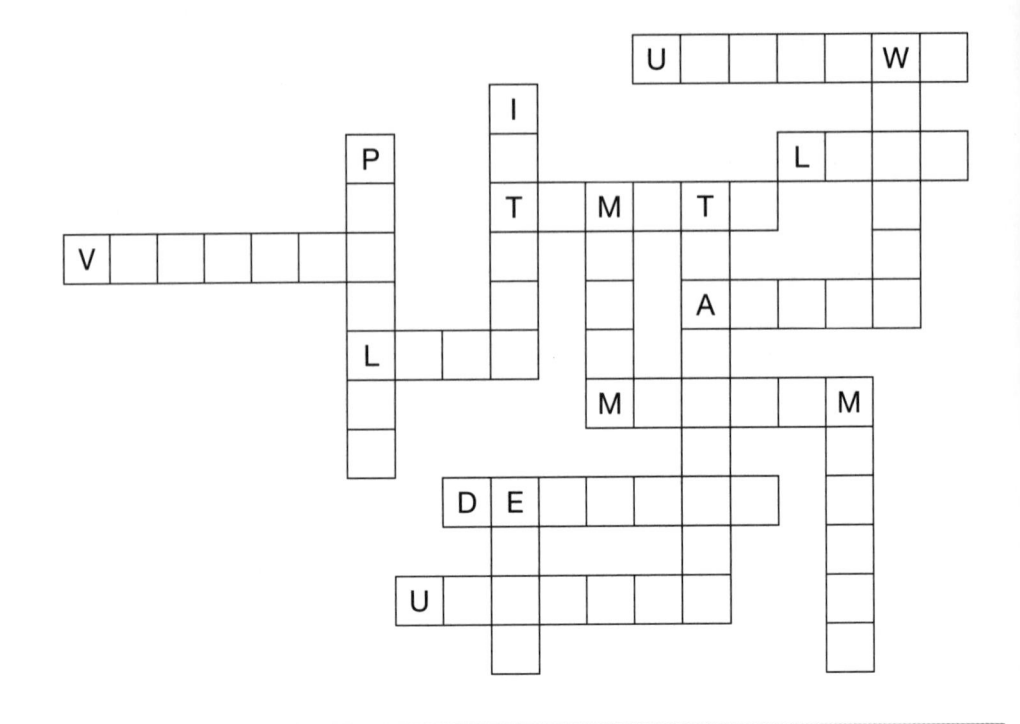

Unit 3

Bond Skills Spelling and Vocabulary 10–11

Album
Develop
Epic
Intern
Lawn
Lisp
Madam
Medium
Museum
Problem
Tomato
Transform
Uniform
Unknown
Volcano
Wisdom

(E) All of the words in your list are hidden in this grid. To help you, the first letter of each word has been given. Can you complete the grid? [16]

(F) Which of your words mean the following? [8]

1   Not large, not small   _____

2   To change   _____

3   A red salad fruit   _____

4   A difficulty   _____

5   Heroic   _____

6   All the same   _____

7   A book of photographs   _____

8   Not familiar   _____

24

Recap

Bond Skills Spelling and Vocabulary 10–11

Unit 4

Ⓐ Once you have found all of the words in your list in the word search, the remaining letters spell out a message that is connected to these words. [17]

1   What is the message? _____

P	E	R	F	O	R	M	A	N	C	E
I	S	O	S	B	E	I	G	S	M	P
C	E	L	I	S	S	S	L	E	U	R
T	R	I	M	E	P	T	A	N	S	E
U	V	V	P	R	O	A	N	S	C	C
R	E	E	L	V	N	K	C	I	L	I
E	A	L	E	E	S	E	E	B	E	S
P	I	M	P	L	E	P	U	L	S	E
I	N	C	L	U	D	E	L	E	E	N
D	I	M	I	R	A	C	L	E	N	E

Ⓑ Can you write the following words backwards and then put these new words into alphabetical order? [10]

sensible   pimple   simple   miracle   muscle

_____   _____   _____   _____   _____

1st _____   2nd _____   3rd _____   4th _____   5th _____

Glance

Include

Miracle

Mistake

Muscle

Observe

Olive

Performance

Picture

Pimple

Precise

Pulse

Response

Sensible

Serve

Simple

27

Unit 4

Bond Skills Spelling and Vocabulary 10–11

Chasing

Coming

Dancing

Firing

Flowing

Hiding

Hoping

Listening

Lying

Making

Shining

Slithering

Staring

Surprising

Trying

Wondering

C What is the root word of these verbs? [16]

1 Dancing _____
2 Flowing _____
3 Coming _____
4 Listening _____
5 Making _____
6 Shining _____
7 Surprising _____
8 Staring _____
9 Chasing _____
10 Hoping _____
11 Hiding _____
12 Lying _____
13 Firing _____
14 Slithering _____
15 Wondering _____
16 Trying _____

D Which of your words fit into the rhyme below so that it makes sense? [4]

1 Learning to skip was tricky, so the girl began crying.
   But the teacher understood that the child was _____ .

2 The kindly, wise teacher who was gentle and caring,
   When she saw the other children were pointing and _____ .

3 Wanted to stop the little girl's panic from rising,
   So the teacher did something that was really _____ .

4 She let the whole class choose either skipping or prancing,
   And then praised the little girl on her beautiful _____ .

20

Bond Skills Spelling and Vocabulary 10–11

Unit 4

E) All of the words in your list are here but the letters have been replaced by numbers. Can you work out which letter each number represents to solve the puzzle? [21]

A		M	
B		N	
C		O	
D		P	
E	22	R	
F		S	
G		T	
H		U	
I		V	
K		W	
L		Y	

Word list:
- Always
- Figures
- Sandals
- Sausage
- Scorch
- Shadow
- Shivered
- Spare
- Spirits
- Stalk
- Standard
- Starve
- Stumble
- Survive
- Swarmed
- System

F) All of these words have at least one 's' at the beginning or end. Seven of the words make another word when we remove an 's'. Can you find the seven words? [7]

1. _____
2. _____
3. _____
4. _____
5. _____
6. _____
7. _____

28

Unit 4

Bond Skills Spelling and Vocabulary 10–11

Ability
Activity
Charity
Discovery
Empty
Envy
Finally
Journey
Nursery
Pansy
Parsley
Penalty
Secondary
Storey
Study
Surely

G) All of the words in your list are hidden in this grid. To help you, the first letter of each word has been given. Can you complete the grid? [16]

H) Which of your words mean the following? [8]

1 A herb   _____

2 A voyage   _____

3 Talent   _____

4 Blank   _____

5 Jealousy   _____

6 A pretty flower   _____

7 Floor level   _____

8 Certainly   _____

24

Recap

Bond Skills Spelling and Vocabulary 10–11

Unit 5

A Can you use a line to join the words in your list to their definitions? [16]

#	Word	Definition
1	Major	A large animal.
2	Minor	A bed cover.
3	Muscular	On our clothes, allowing us to carry things.
4	Scar	A writer.
5	Author	A problem.
6	Burglar	Something really important.
7	Emperor	Something unimportant.
8	Instructor	To draw attention to something.
9	Elegant	To have muscles.
10	Elephant	Your teacher might be lenient or they may be this?
11	Servant	The mark of an old injury.
12	Strict	Someone who serves.
13	Pocket	Someone who steals.
14	Blanket	A coach or teacher.
15	Highlight	A leader of a country.
16	Fault	To be smart or sophisticated.

B Which of your words have these smaller words hidden in them? [8]

1 Leg _____
2 Nor _____
3 Car _____
4 Van _____
5 Lank _____
6 Tor _____
7 In _____
8 Light _____

Author
Blanket
Burglar
Elegant
Elephant
Emperor
Fault
Highlight
Instructor
Major
Minor
Muscular
Pocket
Scar
Servant
Strict

24

Unit 5

Bond Skills Spelling and Vocabulary 10–11

(c) All of the words in your list are here but the letters have been replaced with numbers. Can you work out which letter each number represents to solve the puzzle? [17]

Word list:
- Boulder
- Cough
- Council
- County
- Couple
- Crouch
- Double
- Doubt
- Furious
- Mould
- Mound
- Mourn
- Rough
- Route
- Scout
- Shoulders

Letter key: B, C, D, E (20), F, G, H, I, L, M, N, O, P, R, S, T, U, Y

Helpful Hint

All of these words have 'ou' in them, but look at the different sounds that they make

('o' = cough 'ow' = county 'u' = couple 'O' = boulder 'or' = mourn 'oo' = route).

Can you think of other 'ou' words that share these sounds?

17

Bond Skills Spelling and Vocabulary 10–11

Unit 5

D All of these words are compound words as they are made up of two other words. Can you join the words together to make the compound words? [16]

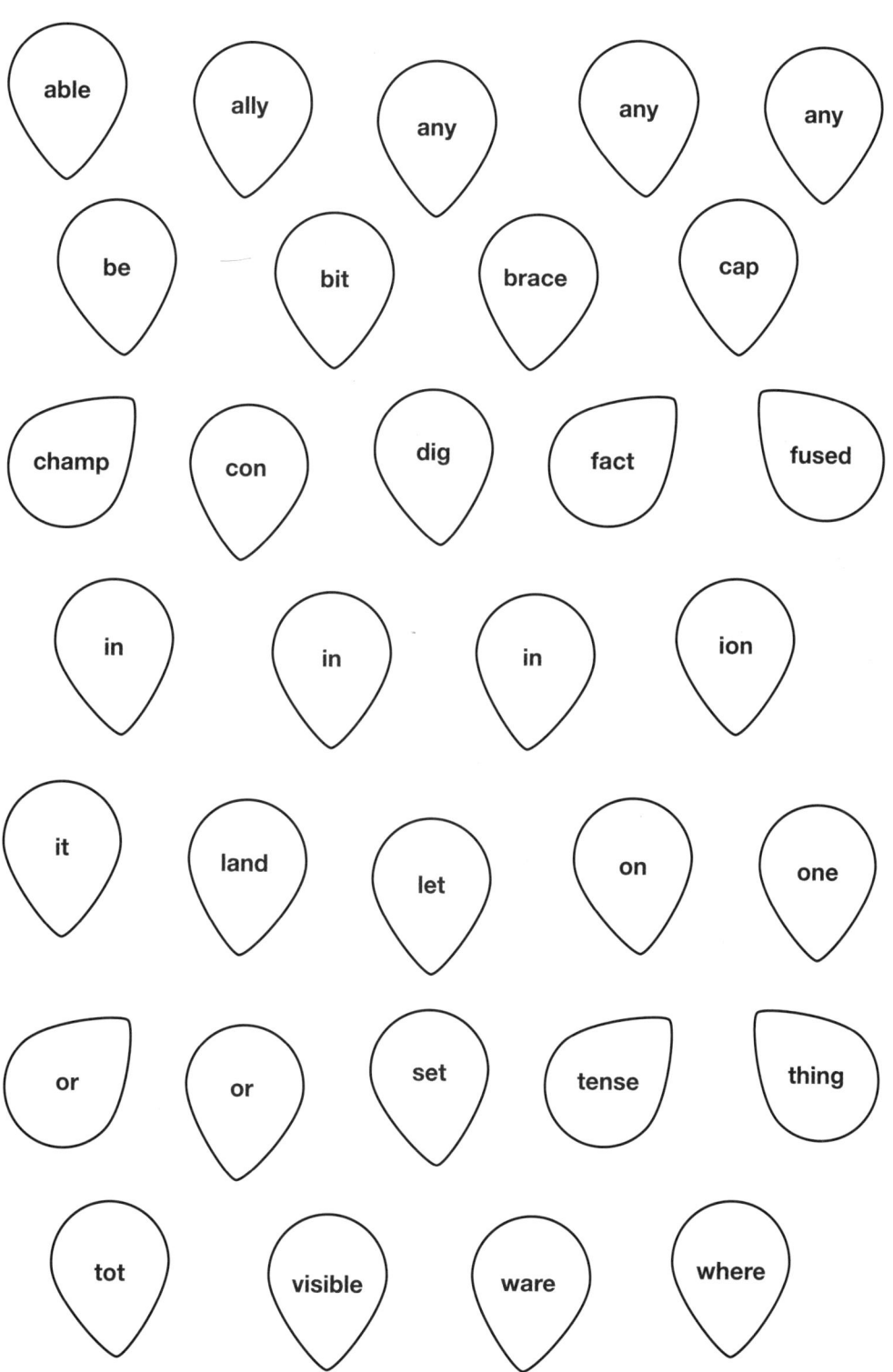

Word parts in teardrops:
able, ally, any, any, any, be, bit, brace, cap, champ, con, dig, fact, fused, in, in, in, ion, it, land, let, on, one, or, or, set, tense, thing, tot, visible, ware, where

Answers:
- Anyone
- Anything
- Anywhere
- Beware
- Bracelet
- Capable
- Champion
- Confused
- Digit
- Factor
- Inland
- Intense
- Invisible
- Onset
- Orbit
- Totally

16

Unit 5

Bond Skills Spelling and Vocabulary 10–11

Debt

Design

Disguise

Gnome

Ghost

Knocked

Knot

Scene

Science

Sighed

Solemn

Tomb

Wrinkle

Writing

Wrong

Yacht

28

E Underline the silent letters that we do not hear in these words. [16]

1 Debt
2 Disguise
3 Ghost
4 Knot
5 Scene
6 Sighed
7 Wrinkle
8 Wrong
9 Design
10 Gnome
11 Knocked
12 Solemn
13 Science
14 Tomb
15 Writing
16 Yacht

F Which of the words in your list fit these definitions? [8]

1 A spectre   _____
2 Serious   _____
3 A boat   _____
4 Breathed   _____
5 Incorrect   _____
6 Crease   _____
7 Pattern   _____
8 Using a pen   _____

G Which of your words rhyme with the words given below? [4]

1 Room   _____
2 Foam   _____
3 Roast   _____
4 Mean   _____

Recap 22

Answers

Bond Skills Spelling and Vocabulary 10–11

Unit 1

A
1. Twirl – To twist or spin.
2. Bridal – Wedding, marriage.
3. Plaits – Braided hair or thread.
4. Blank – A missing space.
5. Grateful – Appreciative.
6. Laundry – Washing.
7. Powerful – Strong.
8. Social – Community or communal.
9. Wonderful – Fantastic.
10. Selfish – Not generous or thoughtful.
11. Claim – To make a statement.
12. Plastic – A material.
13. Uncle – My mother's or father's brother.
14. Style – Fashion.
15. Temple – A place of worship.
16. Lug – Drag, pull, heave.

B
1. Blank
2. Bridal
3. Claim

C

24	15	3	11	8	21	22	10	4	14	5	17	12	18	23	25	7	13	20
A	B	C	D	E	F	G	H	I	L	N	O	P	R	S	T	U	V	W

D
1. ion
2. riot

E
1. brilliant
2. grief
3. alien

F
Across:
2. Query
4. Queue
7. Liquid
8. Glue
11. Fuel
12. Squirrel
14. Biscuits
15. Avenue

Down:
1. Cruel
3. Juice
5. Equator
6. Square
9. Valuable
10. Issue
11. Fluid
13. Rescue

G
1. alter
2. quiver
3. corner
4. crater
5. danger
6. number
7. prefer
8. lobster
9. hover
10. partner
11. customer
12. together
13. splinter
14. helicopter
15. register
16. disaster

H
1. danger
2. splinter
3. customer
4. prefer
5. alter
6. disaster

Unit 2

A
1. **Message:** END WITH 'TION'

B
1. converse
2. decorate
3. describe
4. direct
5. invent
6. celebrate
7. operate
8. protect

C

Crossword answers: COVERED, STUMPED, TORTURED, IMPEDED, PRODUCED, BEDREW, FROWNED, ITCHED, RETURNED, WAN, LINED, SNORED, DODGED, SHED, ENTERED, CAUSED, RED, HAUNTED, CLIMBED

D
1. frowned
2. climbed
3. wandered
4. bothered
5. finished
6. striped
7. returned
8. covered

E

11	1	18	20	3	21	7	10	17	15	26	14	19	6	13	24	22	5
A	B	C	E	G	I	J	K	L	M	N	O	P	R	S	T	U	V

F
1. telescope
2. pause
3. trickle
4. relative
5. visible
6. curve
7. solve/prove
8. voice

G
1. **Message:** THE END LETTER 'D'

H
1. wondered
2. hind
3. wand
4. arid
5. almond
6. answered
7. crowd
8. overjoyed

Unit 3

A
1. gently
2. marriage
3. passenger
4. sponge
5. generous
6. fridge
7. ledge
8. general
9. challenge
10. agile
11. energy
12. carriage
13. garage
14. rampage
15. porridge
16. messenger

B
1. elf
2. family
3. mummy
4. vegetable
5. noise
6. bunny
7. daisy
8. reply
9. enemy
10. lady
11. memory
12. body
13. sense
14. berry
15. soldier
16. oneself

C
1. families or mummies
2. vegetables
3. soldiers
4. berries
5. replies
6. bunnies
7. mummies
8. enemies

Bond Skills Spelling and Vocabulary 10–11

(D) **Across:**
1 German
3 Frozen
6 Unison
8 Chain
9 Italian
13 Orphan
14 Stain
15 Skeleton

Down:
1 Grown
2 Reason
4 Opinion
5 Horizon
7 Fashion
10 Listen
11 Concern
12 Mansion

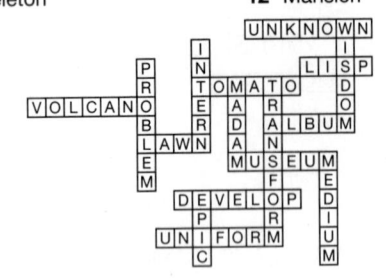

(E) Crossword grid with answers: UNKNOWN, LISP, PROBE, INTO, TOMATO, VOLCANO, EAR, ALBUM, LAWN, MUSEUM, DEVELOP, UNIFORM, MEDIUM

(F)
1 medium
2 transform
3 tomato
4 problem
5 epic
6 uniform
7 album
8 unknown

Unit 4

(A) 1 **Message:** ALL END IN 'E'

(B) 1st elbisnes
2nd elcarim
3rd elcsum
4th elpmip
5th elpmis

(C)
1 dance
2 flow
3 come
4 listen
5 make
6 shine
7 surprise
8 stare
9 chase
10 hope
11 hide
12 lie
13 fire
14 slither
15 wonder
16 try

(D) 1 trying
2 staring
3 surprising
4 dancing

(E)
A	B	C	D	E	F	G	H	I	J	K	L
24	10	14	4	22	13	23	18	8	5	9
M	N	O	P	R	S	T	U	V	W	Y
19	25	17	1	3	7	21	11	2	15	16

(F) 1–7 **In any order:** warmed, sandal, spirit, pare, figure, talk, tumble

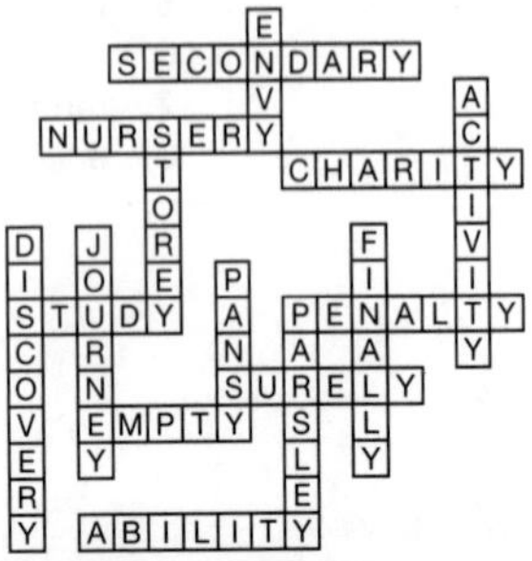

(G) Crossword with answers: SECONDARY, NURSERY, CHARITY, STUDY, PENALTY, SURELY, EMPTY, ABILITY, DISCOVERY, JOURNEY, STORE, PAIN, FINAL, VICTORY

(H)
1 parsley
2 journey
3 ability
4 empty
5 envy
6 pansy
7 storey
8 surely

Unit 5

(A)
1 Major – Something really important.
2 Minor – Something unimportant.
3 Muscular – To have muscles.
4 Scar – The mark of an old injury.
5 Author – A writer.
6 Burglar – Someone who steals.
7 Emperor – A leader of a country.
8 Instructor – A coach or teacher.
9 Elegant – To be smart or sophisticated.
10 Elephant – A large animal.
11 Servant – Someone who serves.
12 Strict – Your teacher might be lenient or they may be this?
13 Pocket – On our clothes allowing us to carry things.
14 Blanket – A bed cover.
15 Highlight – To draw attention to something.
16 Fault – A problem.

(B)
1 elegant
2 minor
3 scar
4 servant
5 blanket
6 instructor
7 minor/instructor
8 highlight

(C)
18	16	23	20	22	10	6	26	24	3	7	17	19	8	13	4	21	11
B	C	D	E	F	G	H	I	L	M	N	O	P	R	S	T	U	Y

(D) **In any order:** Any + one, any + thing, any + where, in + land, in + tense, in + visible, on + set, or + bit, tot + ally, be + ware, brace + let, cap + able, champ + ion, con + fused, dig + it, fact + or

(E)
1 b
2 u
3 h
4 k
5 c
6 gh
7 w
8 w
9 g
10 g
11 k
12 n
13 c
14 b
15 w
16 ch

(F)
1 ghost
2 solemn
3 yacht
4 sighed
5 wrong
6 wrinkle
7 design
8 writing

(G)
1 Tomb
2 Gnome
3 Ghost
4 Scene

Unit 6

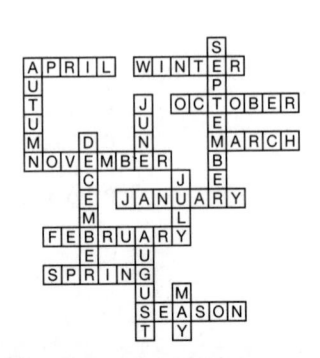

(A) Crossword with answers: APRIL, WINTER, OCTOBER, MARCH, NOVEMBER, JANUARY, FEBRUARY, SPRING, SEASON, AUTUMN, JUNE, JULY, DECEMBER, SUMMER, MAY

Bond Skills Spelling and Vocabulary 10–11

B
1 March
2 October
3 June
4 December
5 July
6 May

C
1 wardrobe
2 mastermind
3 nonsense
4 practice
5 subtract
6 rotate
7 photograph
8 pinstripe
9 purchase
10 theme/slither
11 photocopy
12 slither
13 palace
14 subtract/practice/practise
15 milkshake
16 maybe/wardrobe

D
1 purchase
2 rotate
3 maybe
4 slither
5 subtract
6 nonsense
7 photograph
8 theme
9 wardrobe
10 palace

E

16	23	3	25	10	17	26	12	2	8	18	20	11	14	5	4	1
A	C	D	E	H	I	K	L	M	N	O	P	R	S	T	U	W

F
1 choir
2 kitchen
3 orchard
4 sandwich
5 scheme
6 snatched

G
1 dense
2 estate
3 entrance
4 delicate
5 castle
6 bridge
7 acute
8 hesitate
9 whose
10 distance
11 defence
12 acre
13 ankle
14 amble
15 evidence
16 obstacle

H
1 evidence
2 ankle
3 defence
4 hesitate
5 entrance
6 delicate
7 obstacle
8 dense

Unit 7

A 1 **Message:** WORDS WITH A 'Z', 'Y', 'X'

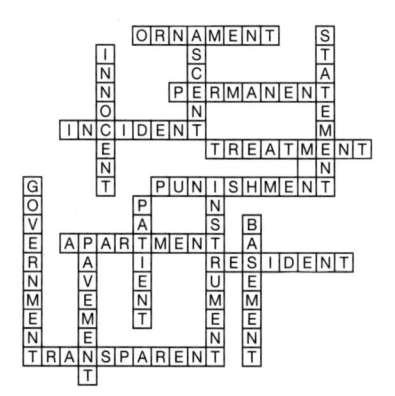

B
1 excuse
2 examine
3 apex
4 wizard
5 expensive
6 expand
7 recognize
8 prize

C [crossword with entries: ORNAMENT, INNOCENT, PERMANENT, INCIDENT, TREATMENT, PUNISHMENT, APARTMENT, RESIDENT, GOVERNMENT, TRANSPARENT]

D
1 permanent
2 punishment
3 innocent
4 ascent
5 transparent
6 resident

E
1 bare
2 rare
3 scale
4 slime
5 strange
6 thirst
7 rapid
8 safe
9 scare
10 sparkle
11 taste
12 true

F
1st ytefas
2nd ytiruces
3rd ytsat
4th ytsriht

G

25	14	2	21	13	15	11	19	9	6	7	5	3	26	1	20	17	24
A	B	C	D	E	F	G	H	I	L	M	N	O	P	R	S	T	U

H
1 trouble
2 glorious
3 tourist
4 poison
5 choice
6 coarse

Unit 8

A **Across:**
4 Expose
5 Fragile
7 Envelope
11 Enclose
12 Phrase
13 Sole
14 Reduce

Down:
1 Grime
2 Stride
3 Dire
4 Explode
6 Ignite
8 Escape
9 Irate
10 Mace
12 Paste

B 1 **Message:** THEY END IN Y

C
1st yadirf
2nd ydaerla
3rd yenom
4th yretsym
5th yreviled

D [crossword with entries: REMOVAL, DECIMAL, SEVERAL, NATIONAL, OFFICIAL, PETROL, HOSTEL, PERSONAL, SPITE, AWFUL, LABEL]

E
1 petrol
2 spiteful
3 parcel
4 personal
5 initial
6 label
7 several
8 official

F
1 nation
2 origin
3 person
4 remove
5 spite

Bond Skills Spelling and Vocabulary 10–11

(G)

25	26	14	12	23	19	6	18	8	22	13
A	C	D	E	F	G	H	I	K	L	M
20	21	4	16	7	15	1	10	11	9	
N	O	P	R	S	T	U	V	X	Y	

(H) 1 nosy
2 exactly
3 lively
4 luckily

Unit 9

(A) 1 dripping
2 hurriedly
3 umbrella
4 surrender
5 blurred
6 dropped
7 horrible/terrible
8 mirror
9 worrying
10 torrent
11 chopped
12 arrival
13 terrible/horrible
14 arrange
15 starry
16 arrested

(B) **Across:**
1 Lilac
4 Departure
8 Iceberg
10 Camera
12 Picnic
13 Harsh
14 Balance
15 Criminal
16 Rigid

Down:
2 Altar
3 Victim
5 Paragraph
6 Adventure
7 Arena
9 Spectacle
11 Earlier

(C) 1 I burst
2 I cling
3 I sleep
4 I spin
5 I dream
6 I seek
7 I stick
8 I bury
9 I creep
10 I fling
11 I slide
12 I sweep
13 I deal
14 I spy
15 I strike

(D) 1 struck
2 sought
3 stuck
4 swept
5 spun
6 slid

(E) 1st tmaerd
2nd tpek
3rd tpels
4th tperc
5th tpews

(F) 1 **Message:** THESE WORDS ALL HAVE A SOFT 'C'

(G) 1 circular
2 fierce
3 novice
4 centimetres
5 cancel
6 excited

Unit 10

(A)

18	26	22	13	12	3	19	6	8	10	15	9	25	24	21	1	23	11	4	7	2
A	C	D	E	G	H	I	K	L	M	N	O	P	Q	R	S	T	U	V	W	Y

(B) 1 crease
2 leader
3 creative
4 dreary
5 searching
6 ease

(C) 1 exist
2 reflect
3 urgent
4 pert
5 robot
6 concert
7 pelt
8 neglect
9 malt
10 abduct
11 trust
12 market
13 secret
14 perfect
15 result
16 portrait

(D) 1 urgent
2 result
3 market
4 portrait
5 perfect
6 concert
7 trust
8 reflect

(E) 1 exit
2 mat
3 pet
4 rust

(F) **Across:**
1 Allowed
3 Blossom
5 Assume
7 Stunned
9 Assure
10 Willow
12 Traveller
13 Bullying
14 Cannot

Down:
1 Assist
2 Assent
3 Beginning
4 Tunnel
6 Jewellery
8 Swollen
11 Ballet

(G) [Crossword with answers: SCRIBBLE, DRAGGED, ATTIC, LITTLE, MASSIVE, STAGGERN, SNAPPED, BATTERED, OTTER, RECOMMEND, FORGOTTEN, BANNER, IMMENSE, JAGGED]

(H) 1 batter
2 drag
3 stab
4 mass
5 chat
6 snap
7 forget
8 scribe

Bond Skills Spelling and Vocabulary 10–11   **Unit 6**

A All of the words in your list are hidden in this grid. To help you, the first letter of each word has been given. Can you complete the grid? [16]

April

August

Autumn

December

February

January

July

June

March

May

November

October

Season

September

Spring

Winter

B The months of the year are named after words that are sometimes names, sometimes numbers. Can you work out which month fits each definition? [6]

1   Mars, the Roman god of war   _____

2   This was the 8th month   _____

3   Juno, the Roman goddess of marriage _____

4   This was the 10th month   _____

5   Julius Caesar, Roman leader   _____

6   Maia, goddess of spring   _____

22

Unit 6

Bond Skills Spelling and Vocabulary 10–11

Mastermind

Maybe

Milkshake

Nonsense

Palace

Photocopy

Photograph

Pinstripe

Practice

Practise

Purchase

Rotate

Slither

Subtract

Theme

Wardrobe

C) Which of the words in your list have these little words in them? [16]

1 Rob _____
2 Term _____
3 On   _____
4 Ice _____
5 Sub _____
6 Ate _____
7 Tog _____
8 Rip _____
9 Has _____
10 The _____
11 Cop _____
12 Lit _____
13 Ace _____
14 Act _____
15 Hake _____
16 Be   _____

D) Which of your words fits these descriptions? [10]

1 To buy   _____
2 To turn   _____
3 Possibly   _____
4 Slide   _____
5 To take away   _____
6 Rubbish   _____
7 A camera picture   _____
8 Topic or title   _____
9 A clothes cupboard _____
10 Royal home   _____

💡 **Helpful Hint**

A quick way of remembering when to use practice ('c') and practise ('s') is that the noun uses practice ('c') while the verb uses the 's' (for spellings) so I PRACTISE my SPELLINGS.

26

Bond Skills Spelling and Vocabulary 10–11

Unit 6

E All of the words in your list are here but the letters have been replaced by numbers. Can you work out which letter each number represents to solve the puzzle? [16]

A	
C	
D	
E	
H	
I	
K	
L	
M	
N	
O	
P	
R	
S	14
T	
U	
W	

Word list:
- Ached
- Character
- Chocolates
- Choir
- Choked
- Chucked
- Kitchen
- Launch
- Machines
- Orchard
- Pitched
- Sandwich
- Scheme
- Snatched
- Stitched
- Stomach

F Which of your words fit these descriptions? [6]

1. A group of singers _____
2. A room we cook in _____
3. A group of fruit trees _____
4. A bread snack _____
5. A plot or plan _____
6. Pinched _____

22

Unit 6

Bond Skills Spelling and Vocabulary 10–11

Acre
Acute
Amble
Ankle
Bridge
Castle
Defence
Delicate
Dense
Distance
Entrance
Estate
Evidence
Hesitate
Obstacle
Whose

(G) All of the words in your list end in 'e' but they are all jumbled up. Can you turn these anagrams into their proper words? [16]

1 Sende   _____
2 Teesat   _____
3 Catneren   _____
4 Lacetide   _____
5 Lacest   _____
6 Grideb   _____
7 Caute   _____
8 Asheetti   _____
9 Sheow   _____
10 Dancesit   _____
11 Feedcen   _____
12 Care   _____
13 Klean   _____
14 Blame   _____
15 Diveceen   _____
16 Lobescat   _____

(H) Which of your words fit these descriptions? [8]

1 Proof   _____
2 Part of the leg _____
3 Protection   _____
4 Falter   _____
5 Arrival   _____
6 Fragile   _____
7 Hurdle   _____
8 Thick, solid   _____

Recap

Bond Skills Spelling and Vocabulary 10–11

Unit 7

A Once you have found all of the words in your list in the word search, the remaining letters spell out a message that is connected to these words. [17]

1 What is the message? _____

W	I	Z	A	R	D	P	R	I	Z	E
Y	E	X	P	E	N	S	I	V	E	X
O	X	E	X	P	L	O	R	E	W	I
K	A	X	E	X	E	C	U	T	E	S
E	M	P	X	O	Y	O	G	A	R	T
Y	I	A	C	J	A	Z	Z	P	D	E
O	N	N	U	S	W	W	I	E	T	N
L	E	D	S	H	N	A	Z	X	Y	C
K	X	R	E	C	O	G	N	I	Z	E

B Which of your words have a similar meaning to the words here? [8]

1 Reason _____

2 Inspect _____

3 Top _____

4 Warlock _____

5 Dear _____

6 Increase _____

7 Identify _____

8 Award _____

Apex

Examine

Excuse

Execute

Expand

Existence

Expensive

Explore

Jazz

Prize

Recognize

Wizard

Yawn

Yoga

Yoke

Yolk

25

Unit 7

Bond Skills Spelling and Vocabulary 10–11

Apartment
Ascent
Basement
Government
Incident
Innocent
Instrument
Ornament
Patient
Pavement
Permanent
Punishment
Resident
Statement
Transparent
Treatment

22

c) All of the words in your list are hidden in this grid. To help you, the first letter of each word has been given. Can you complete the grid? [16]

d) Which of your words are opposites of these words? [6]

1   Temporary   _____

2   Reward   _____

3   Guilty   _____

4   Descent   _____

5   Opaque   _____

6   Visitor   _____

Unit 7

Bond Skills Spelling and Vocabulary 10–11

E What is the root of these words? [12]

1. Barely _____
2. Rarely _____
3. Scaly _____
4. Slimy _____
5. Strangely _____
6. Thirsty _____
7. Rapidly _____
8. Safety _____
9. Scary _____
10. Sparkly _____
11. Tasty _____
12. Truly _____

F Can you write the following words backwards and then put these new words into alphabetical order? [8]

| thirsty | tasty | security | safety |

_____   _____   _____   _____

1st _____   2nd _____   3rd _____   4th _____

Helpful Hint

All of these words end in 'y'. When we add a 'y' to the end of a word, we usually remove the final 'e' first. Scale = scaly, scare = scary, slime = slimy, taste = tasty. Can you think of other words that follow this same spelling pattern?

Barely
Fancy
Fury
Rapidly
Rarely
Safety
Satisfy
Scaly
Scary
Security
Slimy
Sparkly
Strangely
Tasty
Thirsty
Truly

20

Unit 7

Bond Skills Spelling and Vocabulary 10–11

Boarding

Choice

Coarse

Dominoes

Glorious

Loaf

Poison

Serious

Soar

Soul

Source

Thoughtful

Thousands

Throughout

Tourist

Trouble

/23

(G) All of the words in your list are here but the letters have been replaced by numbers. Can you work out which letter each number represents to solve the puzzle? [17]

T 17

(H) Which of your words mean the same as these words? [6]

1 Problem _____

2 Wonderful _____

3 Visitor _____

4 Toxin _____

5 Option _____

6 Rough _____

Recap   34

Bond Skills Spelling and Vocabulary 10–11

Unit 8

A All of the words in your list are hidden in this grid. Can you solve the clues to complete the grid? [16]

Across

4 Uncover
5 Delicate
7 For transporting a letter
11 Surround
12 Idiom, expression
13 Part of the foot
14 Lessen

Down

1 Dirt
2 Step
3 Awful
4 Blow up
6 Set on fire
8 Flee
9 Angry
10 Weapon
12 Glue

Dire
Enclose
Envelope
Escape
Explode
Expose
Fragile
Grime
Ignite
Irate
Mace
Paste
Phrase
Reduce
Sole
Stride

16

Unit 8

Bond Skills Spelling and Vocabulary 10–11

Already
Delivery
Destroy
Friday
Heavy
Holiday
Literacy
Military
Monday
Money
Mystery
Saturday
Sunday
Thursday
Tuesday
Wednesday

B Once you have found all of the words in your list in the word search, the remaining letters spell out a message that relates to your words. [17]

1 What is the message? _____

L	T	M	S	U	N	D	A	Y	H	E	H	W
I	M	I	A	D	E	S	T	R	O	Y	O	E
T	O	L	T	H	U	R	S	D	A	Y	L	D
E	N	I	U	H	E	A	V	Y	Y	E	I	N
R	D	T	R	M	O	N	E	Y	N	D	D	E
A	A	A	D	E	L	I	V	E	R	Y	A	S
C	Y	R	A	L	R	E	A	D	Y	I	Y	D
Y	N	Y	Y	M	Y	S	T	E	R	Y	Y	A
F	R	I	D	A	Y	T	U	E	S	D	A	Y

C Can you write the following words backwards and then place these new words in alphabetical order? [10]

Friday   mystery   delivery   already   money

1st _____ 2nd _____ 3rd _____ 4th _____ 5th _____

27

Bond Skills Spelling and Vocabulary 10–11

Unit 8

D All of the words in your list are hidden in this grid. To help you, the first letter of each word has been given. Can you complete the grid? [16]

Awful

Control

Decimal

Dismal

Hostel

Initial

Label

National

Official

Original

Parcel

Personal

Petrol

Removal

Several

Spiteful

E Which of your words are most similar to the words here? [8]

1 Fuel _____   5 First _____

2 Mean _____   6 Sticker _____

3 Package _____   7 Many _____

4 Individual _____ 8 Certified _____

F What are the root words of the following words? [5]

1 National _____   4 Removal _____

2 Original _____   5 Spiteful _____

3 Personal _____

29

Unit 8

Bond Skills Spelling and Vocabulary 10–11

Angrily

Costly

Dingy

Exactly

Excitedly

Floury

Guilty

Happily

Lively

Lonely

Lovely

Luckily

Nasty

Normally

Nosy

Rosy

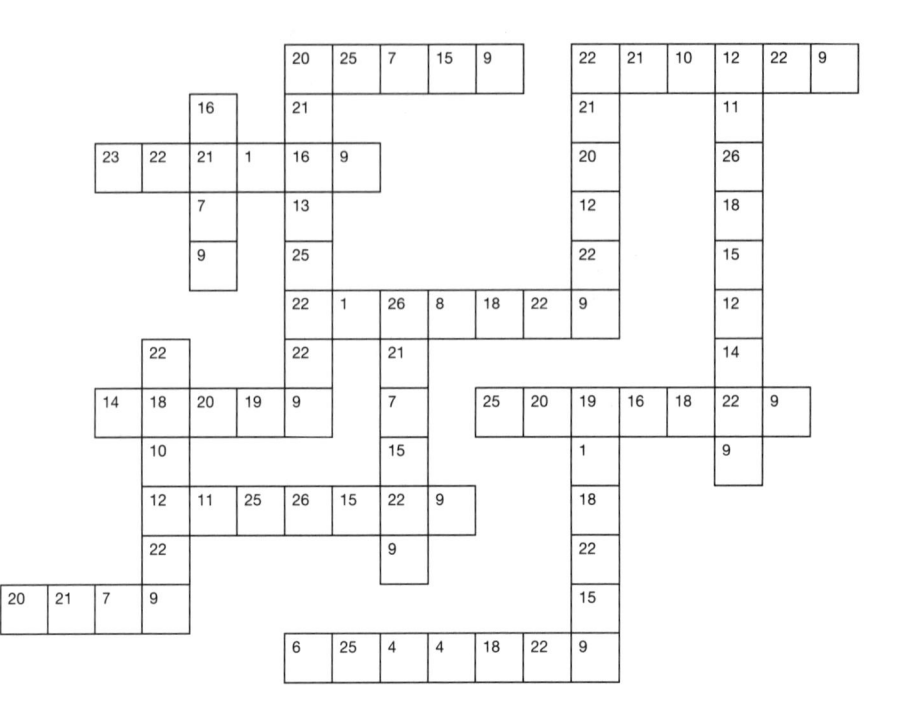

(G) All of the words in your list are here but the letters have been replaced by numbers. Can you work out which letter each number represents to solve the puzzle? [20]

| A | C | D | E | F | G | H | I | K | L | M | N | O | P | R | S | T | U | V | X | Y |

(Position 19 is highlighted above the letter grid.)

(H) Which of your words fit these descriptions? [4]

1   Curious   _____

2   A precise amount _____

3   Animated   _____

4   Fortunately   _____

Helpful Hint

All of these words end in 'y'. If you see a word ending in 'ly' it is usually an adverb as it describes how something is done (ran quickly); but words ending in 'ly' can also be adjectives as they describe the noun (costly mistake).

Recap

Unit 9

Bond Skills Spelling and Vocabulary 10–11

A Can you place one of the words in your list into the spaces below so that the sentences make sense? [16]

1. We need a plumber to stop that tap from _____ .
2. We _____ raced to the bus stop hoping not to be too late.
3. I need my _____ today as it is raining and I shall be outdoors.
4. The British commander had to _____ and his army retreated.
5. After the optician put eye drops in, my eyesight was _____ .
6. He _____ the ball before running away.
7. Having toothache was _____ as I couldn't enjoy the party.
8. Grandma saw her new hairstyle in the _____ and smiled.
9. It was no good _____ about his exam results.
10. The little brook broke its bank as the _____ of water flooded the land.
11. My eyes watered as I _____ the onions.
12. The Queen's _____ at the palace was watched by the crowds.
13. It was _____ to hear of the homes that had been flooded.
14. Could we _____ to meet up next weekend?
15. The cold, _____ night sky was so clear and bright.
16. The police _____ the woman who was breaking in to the house.

Arrange
Arrested
Arrival
Blurred
Chopped
Dripping
Dropped
Horrible
Hurriedly
Mirror
Starry
Surrender
Terrible
Torrent
Umbrella
Worrying

Helpful Hint

All of these words have double letters in them. If a word has two syllables, it often has a double consonant (arrest, arrange). If a word ends with a single consonant with a single vowel before it, the consonant is often doubled before we add a suffix (drip–dripping).

Unit 9

Bond Skills Spelling and Vocabulary 10–11

Adventure
Altar
Arena
Balance
Camera
Criminal
Departure
Earlier
Harsh
Iceberg
Lilac
Paragraph
Picnic
Rigid
Spectacle
Victim

B All of the words in your list are hidden in this grid. Can you solve the clues to complete the grid? [16]

Across

1. A purple colour
4. Leaving
8. A huge block of ice
10. Used in photography
12. A meal outdoors
13. Cruel
14. To create equality
15. An offender
16. Inflexible

Down

2. A raised area in a church
3. A casualty
5. Groups our sentences into chunks
6. An exciting experience
7. Stadium
9. A vision
11. Previously

16

Bond Skills Spelling and Vocabulary 10–11

Unit 9

C All of the words in your list are in the past tense. Can you write them now in the present tense using 'I' at the front of each word? [15]

	Kept	_I keep_	8	Buried	_____
1	Burst	_____	9	Crept	_____
2	Clung	_____	10	Flung	_____
3	Slept	_____	11	Slid	_____
4	Spun	_____	12	Swept	_____
5	Dreamt	_____	13	Dealt	_____
6	Sought	_____	14	Spied	_____
7	Stuck	_____	15	Struck	_____

D Which of your words are most similar to the words here? [6]

1	Hit	_____	4	Brushed	_____
2	Searched	_____	5	Rotated	_____
3	Glued	_____	6	Glided	_____

E Can you write these words backwards and then put them into alphabetical order? [10]

crept   slept   swept   kept   dreamt

_____ _____ _____ _____ _____

1st _____ 2nd _____ 3rd _____ 4th _____ 5th _____

Buried
Burst
Crept
Clung
Dealt
Dreamt
Flung
Kept
Slept
Slid
Sought
Spied
Spun
Struck
Stuck
Swept

31

Unit 9

Bond Skills Spelling and Vocabulary 10–11

Acid

Ascend

Cancel

Centimetres

Central

Ceremony

Certificate

Circular

Circus

Cities

Citizen

Except

Excited

Fierce

Novice

Silence

23

(F) Once you have found all of the words in your list in the word search, the remaining letters spell out a message that relates to your words. [17]

1   What is the message? _____

C	E	N	T	I	M	E	T	R	E	S	T	C
I	C	O	C	C	A	X	F	H	X	I	E	E
R	A	V	I	I	S	C	I	A	C	L	C	N
C	N	I	T	R	C	E	E	C	I	E	I	T
U	C	C	I	C	E	P	R	I	T	N	T	R
L	E	E	E	U	N	T	C	D	E	C	I	A
A	L	S	S	S	D	E	E	W	D	E	Z	L
R	C	E	R	E	M	O	N	Y	O	R	E	D
C	E	R	T	I	F	I	C	A	T	E	N	S
A	L	L	H	A	V	E	A	S	O	F	T	C

(G) Which of your words fits these descriptions? [6]

1   In a round shape   _____

2   Vicious   _____

3   Beginner   _____

4   Units of measurement   _____

5   Abandon   _____

6   Enthusiastic   _____

💡 **Helpful Hint**

All of these words have a soft 'c' sound, so when you sound out a word and hear the 's' sound, bear in mind that it might be a 'c' creating it!

Recap

Bond Skills Spelling and Vocabulary 10–11

Unit 10

A All of the words in your list are here but the letters have been replaced by numbers. Can you work out which letter each number represents to solve the puzzle? [20]

A	
C	26
D	
E	
G	
H	
I	
K	
L	
M	
N	
O	
P	
Q	
R	
S	
T	
U	
V	
W	
Y	

Creaky

Crease

Creative

Creature

Dreary

Earthquake

Ease

Leader

Leather

Meadow

People

Plead

Please

Repeat

Searching

Spread

26

B Which of your words are most opposite to the words here? [6]

1 Smooth _____

2 Follower _____

3 Unimaginative _____

4 Exciting _____

5 Finding _____

6 Difficulty _____

43

Unit 10

Bond Skills Spelling and Vocabulary 10–11

Abduct

Concert

Exist

Malt

Market

Neglect

Pelt

Perfect

Pert

Portrait

Reflect

Result

Robot

Secret

Trust

Urgent

28

C) All of the words in your list end in the letter 't' but here they are in anagram form. Can you rearrange the letters to find all of your words? [16]

1 Stixe   _____   9   Lamt   _____

2 Clefter _____   10 Badcut _____

3 Grunte _____   11 Strut   _____

4 Trep   _____   12 Tramek _____

5 Bootr   _____   13 Recets _____

6 Cotcren _____   14 Feecptr _____

7 Lept   _____   15 Lurest _____

8 Clenget _____   16 Partriot _____

D) Which of your words fit the descriptions given here? [8]

1 Something very important   _____

2 The final answer   _____

3 Some outdoor shops   _____

4 A picture of a person   _____

5 Ideal   _____

6 Performance   _____

7 To have faith in   _____

8 To mirror   _____

E) Can you take one letter away from the following words to make another word? [4]

1 Exist   _____   3 Pelt   _____

2 Malt   _____   4 Trust   _____

44

Unit 10

Bond Skills Spelling and Vocabulary 10–11

F All of the words in your list are hidden in this grid. Can you use the clues below to help you to complete the grid? [16]

Across
1. Permitted
3. Bloom
5. Suppose
7. Amazed
9. Guarantee
10. A tree
12. Someone who travels
13. Intimidating
14. The opposite of 'can'

Down
1. Help
2. Agree
3. Starting
4. Channel
6. Rings, necklace, earrings?
8. Enlarged
11. A dance

Allowed

Assent

Assist

Assume

Assure

Ballet

Beginning

Blossom

Bullying

Cannot

Jewellery

Stunned

Swollen

Traveller

Tunnel

Willow

16

Unit 10

Bond Skills Spelling and Vocabulary 10–11

Attic

Battered

Chatting

Dragged

Forgotten

Immense

Jagged

Litter

Luggage

Massive

Otter

Pattern

Recommend

Scribble

Snapped

Stabbed

(G) All of the words in your list are hidden in this grid. To help you, the first letter of each word has been given. Can you complete the grid? [16]

(H) What are the roots of these words? [8]

1 Battered _____
2 Dragged _____
3 Stabbed _____
4 Massive _____

5 Chatting _____
6 Snapped _____
7 Forgotten _____
8 Scribble _____

24

Recap

Bond Skills Spelling and Vocabulary 10–11

Unit 2

(A) **Left-over letters spell:** END WITH 'TION'

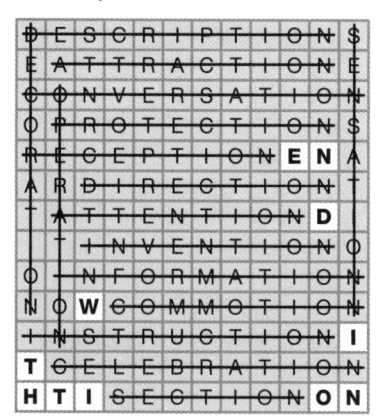

(G) **Left-over letters spell:** THE END LETTER 'D'

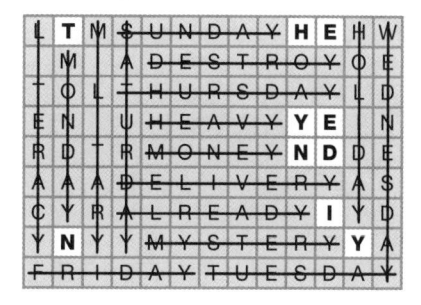

Unit 4

(A) **Left-over letters spell:** ALL END IN 'E'

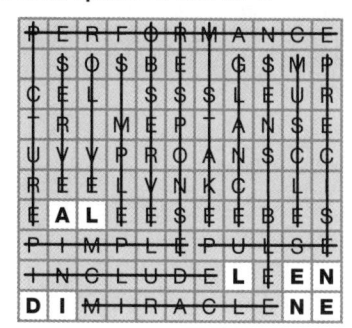

Unit 7

(A) **Left-over letters spell:** WORDS WITH A 'Z', 'Y', 'X'

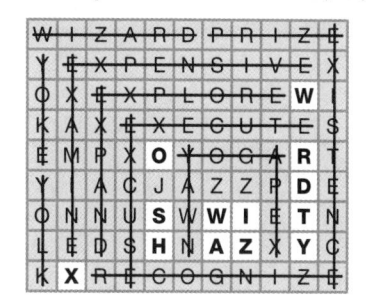

Unit 8

(B) **Left-over letters spell:** THEY END IN 'Y'

Unit 9

(F) **Left-over letters spell:** THESE WORDS ALL HAVE A SOFT 'C'

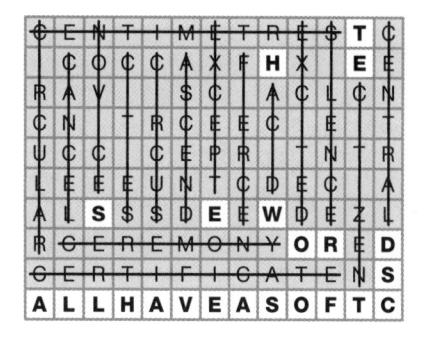

WORD SEARCH SOLUTIONS

Progress Chart

Bond Skills Spelling and Vocabulary 10–11

How did you do? Fill in your score below and shade in the corresponding boxes to compare your progress across the different tests and units.

| | 50% | 100% | | 50% | 100% |

Unit 1, p3 Score: __ / 19

Unit 1, p4 Score: __ / 23

Unit 1, p5 Score: __ / 16

Unit 1, p6 Score: __ / 22

Unit 2, p7 Score: __ / 25

Unit 2, p8 Score: __ / 24

Unit 2, p9 Score: __ / 25

Unit 2, p10 Score: __ / 25

Unit 3, p11 Score: __ / 16

Unit 3, p12 Score: __ / 24

Unit 3, p13 Score: __ / 16

Unit 3, p14 Score: __ / 24

Unit 4, p15 Score: __ / 27

Unit 4, p16 Score: __ / 20

Unit 4, p17 Score: __ / 28

Unit 4, p18 Score: __ / 24

Unit 5, p19 Score: __ / 24

Unit 5, p20 Score: __ / 17

Unit 5, p21 Score: __ / 16

Unit 5, p22 Score: __ / 28

Unit 6, p27 Score: __ / 22

Unit 6, p28 Score: __ / 26

Unit 6, p29 Score: __ / 22

Unit 6, p30 Score: __ / 24

Unit 7, p31 Score: __ / 25

Unit 7, p32 Score: __ / 22

Unit 7, p33 Score: __ / 20

Unit 7, p34 Score: __ / 23

Unit 8, p35 Score: __ / 16

Unit 8, p36 Score: __ / 27

Unit 8, p37 Score: __ / 29

Unit 8, p38 Score: __ / 24

Unit 9, p39 Score: __ / 16

Unit 9, p40 Score: __ / 16

Unit 9, p41 Score: __ / 31

Unit 9, p42 Score: __ / 23

Unit 10, p43 Score: __ / 26

Unit 10, p44 Score: __ / 28

Unit 10, p45 Score: __ / 16

Unit 10, p46 Score: __ / 24